Slugs and Snails

CLAIRE LLEWELLYN • BARRIE WATTS

W
FRANKLIN WATTS
A Division of Scholastic Inc.
NEW YORK TORONTO LONDON AUCKLAND SYDNEY
MEXICO CITY NEW DELHI HONG KONG
DANBURY, CONNECTICUT

First published in 2001 by Franklin Watts
96 Leonard Street, London EC2A 4XD

First American edition 2002 by Franklin Watts
A Division of Scholastic Inc.
90 Sherman Turnpike
Danbury, CT 06816

Series Editor: Anderley Moore
Editor: Rosalind Beckman
Series Designer: Jason Anscomb
Designer: Joelle Wheelwright
Illustrator: David Burroughs

Catalog details are available from the Library of Congress
Cataloging-in-Publication Data

ISBN 0-531-14655-3 (lib. bdg.) 0-531-14828-9 (pbk.)

Printed in Hong Kong/China

Contents

What Are Slugs and Snails?

Slugs and snails belong to a large family of animals called mollusks.

A mollusk is a creature with a soft, slimy body, which is often protected by a shell.

Slugs and snails are very alike. The big difference between them is that snails have shells and slugs do not.

More than half of all slugs and snails live in the sea. The others live in freshwater rivers and ponds, or in shady places on land.

Compare the size of the garden snail (top) with its huge African relative.

There are over 60,000 different kinds of slugs and snails. Some of them are too small to see. Others are as long as your arm.

◀*Most slugs are not very pretty. Some are colorful, like this sea slug from Florida.*

Where They Live

Slugs and snails live in many places. Some live in the woods, where there is always food and shelter.

Grove snails can cling to rocky hillsides or steep cliffs. ▼

▲ *Slugs live in grassy meadows.*

▲ *The great pond snail lives at the bottom of ponds.*

Slugs and snails are easy to find in gardens and parks. They come out when it is cool, early in the morning or late at night. They also come out after a shower of rain. During the day, they hide under trees and bushes, among fallen leaves, or under piles of rocks or garbage.

Slugs have no shells, so they can squeeze under loose bark or burrow into the ground.

In the daytime, snails rest against walls and fences or hide inside pots and under stones.

The Body

Slugs and snails have very similar bodies. The soft, rubbery part is called the foot. It is covered with a sticky coat of slime. This helps the animal move and cling onto windows and walls.

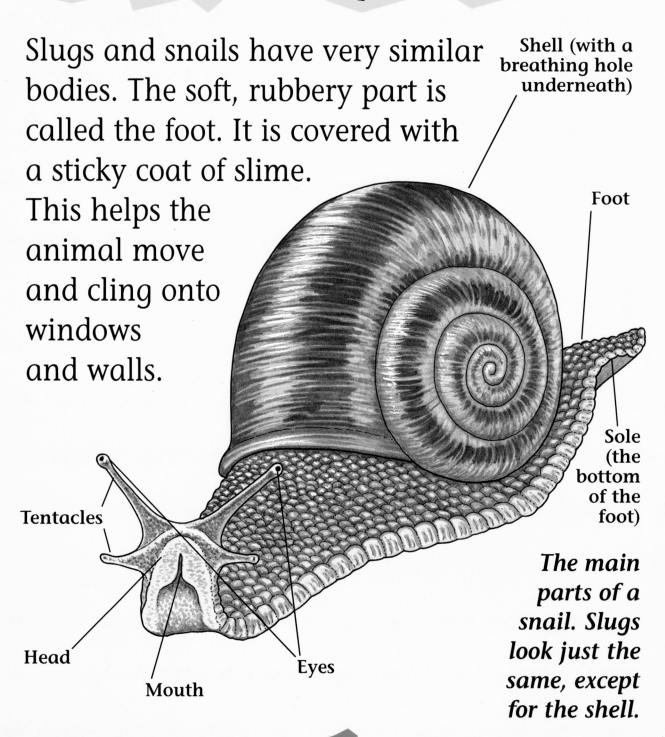

Shell (with a breathing hole underneath)

Foot

Sole (the bottom of the foot)

Tentacles

Head

Mouth

Eyes

The main parts of a snail. Slugs look just the same, except for the shell.

The mantle is a thick fold of skin on top of the foot. It has a small breathing hole that can open and close. In snails, the mantle helps build the shell.

A close-up of a slug's mantle, showing the breathing hole

Slugs and snails have two pairs of tentacles on their heads. At the end of the longer pair are tiny eyes. The shorter pair picks up smells and tastes.

Moving Along

Slugs and snails move by swimming along on a smooth layer of slime. Slime makes it much easier to move on rough ground. The slime also protects the sole of the foot from getting torn.

These silvery slime trails show where slugs have been.

Slugs and snails leave silver trails behind them. These trails show up in the morning, before they have dried up and disappeared.

Slugs and snails creep along on the sole of their feet. Muscles in the foot ripple forward to lift each part of the body. The animal glides along.

A slug leaves its trail on a leaf.

The sole of a snail's foot

Most snails move at about 33 feet per hour. It would take a snail more than 6 years to travel from New York City to Cleveland, Ohio!

A Snail's Shell

A snail builds its own shell. As the snail gets older, its shell grows bigger. The mantle makes new layers of shell and adds them to the end. The new shell is thin and brittle at first, but it quickly hardens.

As it grows bigger, the shell curls around in a spiral called a whorl.

Snail shells can be tall and narrow, or short and wide. They can be smooth and glossy, or rough and dull. Most shells have colored flecks or stripes, but some are plain.

A snail can pull its whole foot inside its shell. This protects it from enemies. It also keeps its body moist when the weather is cold or very dry.

The brightly-colored shell of a Cuban snail ▶

◀ *This shell from a Caribbean snail is shaped just like a peanut.*

This African snail has a sharp, spiny shell. ▶

◀ *The ridged shell of snails found in Europe, Africa, and India.*

Feeding

Most slugs and snails feed on animal droppings, fungi, and dead animals and plants. They eat by rubbing their food with a long, narrow tongue called a radula.

The radula works like a cheese grater. It is covered with rows of tiny teeth that shred the solid food.

The tip of the radula is always wearing out and breaking off. This is okay because the other end never stops growing.

Some slugs and snails are pests in gardens and on farms. They chew holes in green plants and can destroy young seedlings. They eat soft berries and other fruit, or spoil it with their slime.

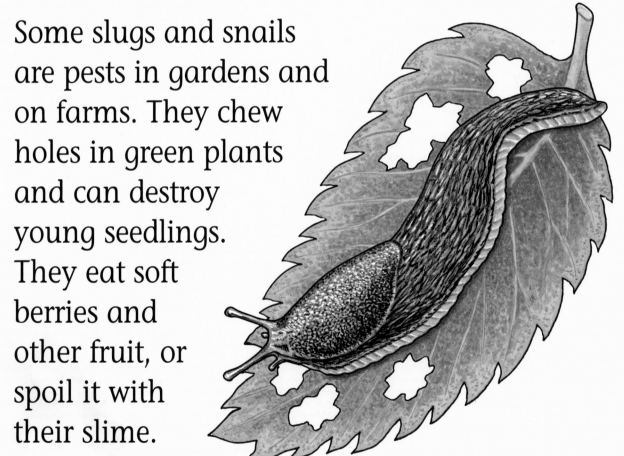

Slugs destroy plants by chewing holes in them.

Mating

Slugs and snails do not have to mate to have young. Most of them have both male and female parts on their body, so they can make eggs on their own. They still prefer to find a mate, though.

Slugs and snails usually mate in the summer. These two slugs make a lot of slime and then lie very close to one another.
▼

A few weeks after mating, both animals lay their eggs. Eggs are laid mostly in the summer and fall. In the fall there is less danger of the eggs drying up.

Slugs and snails lay between twenty and one hundred eggs. The eggs lie hidden in soil, among dead leaves, or under logs and stones.

▲
The eggs look like tiny balls. Some are soft and clear. Others have a chalky white shell.

Growing Up

Slug and snail eggs hatch in batches. The first batch hatches in about three weeks. The next batch hatches a month or two later. More batches hatch as time goes on. Sometimes a whole batch of hatchlings is eaten by enemies or killed by dry weather. Spreading the hatching in batches gives the young a better chance to survive.

▲

These eggs are ready to hatch.

The newly-hatched slugs and snails look just like their parents. They grow quickly as they feed. Most are fully grown by the end of a year. The largest kinds take up to four years.

Many slugs and snails die before they are able to lay eggs of their own. Only five eggs in one hundred will survive to become an adult.

Some slugs and snails live for fifty years, but most of them have very short lives. They end up as meals for other animals.

▲
A newly-hatched snail

Enemies

Slugs have many enemies. They are eaten by hedgehogs, shrews, frogs, toads, worms, and some fierce beetles. All these animals are a gardener's friends because they help bring down the number of slugs.

A frog enjoys its meal of slugs.

Many snails are eaten by birds. Some birds have learned to break the shell and get at the snail inside.

A blackbird can easily smash a shell with its beak.
▼

The song thrush uses a stone to break a snail's shell.

▼

Birds do not like a snail's sticky slime because it gums up their beak. They wipe the body on the ground before eating it.

A Long Rest

In the winter, snails and slugs take a long rest. This is called hibernation. The plants they need for food and shelter die in the cold weather. Snails and slugs sleep so they can survive.

Snails often hibernate in clusters. They become active in the spring, when the air starts getting warm. ▼

In some parts of the world, snails take a summer nap to survive long spells of hot, dry weather. Some snails in California have slept for eight years!

To protect themselves in the winter, snails tuck their feet inside their shells and seal the door with slime. The slime soon dries as hard as leather. Water cannot escape from the animal's body.

▲
A sealed snail shell.

◀ *Slugs burrow into the soil or under logs or stones during the winter.*

Snail and Slug Surprises

Most water snails take in oxygen from the water. Some can also come up to the surface and breathe oxygen in the air.

Snails are strong. They can lift ten times their own weight. That is like a person carrying twenty big sacks of potatoes.

Some people enjoy eating snails cooked with butter and garlic. They use a special fork to get the snail out of the shell.

Slug and snail races are popular. The world's fastest racer is the banana slug, which crawls at about 2 miles per hour.

A snail from Brazil has the world's longest shell. It is 4 inches long, about twice as long as your thumb.

In 1846, a "dead" desert snail had spent four years glued to a display board in the Natural History Museum in London. It woke up and began to feed! The snail lived for another two years.

The largest snail is the African giant snail. It measures up to 15 inches, as long as your arm. Its shell measures over 11 inches, about as long as this book. The giant snail weighs the same as a big bag of sugar.

Most garden snails live for about two years. People keep track of them by numbering their shells with a pen.

Glossary

foot	the soft, rubbery part of a slug or snail's body
hibernation	a long winter sleep that helps animals survive in cold weather
mantle	the thick fold of skin on a slug or snail's body
mollusk	a family of animals with soft, slimy bodies, which are often protected by shells
muscle	a part of an animal's body that helps it move
radula	the tongue of a slug or snail
sole	the bottom of a slug or snail's foot
tentacle	one of the four horns on a slug or snail's head
whorl	the shape of the coils in a snail's shell

Index